TAKING UP THE SERPENT

JERALD BULLIS

Taking up
the Serpent

an Ithaca House book

ithaca

Grateful acknowledgement is due the editors of the following magazines for first publishing the poems listed:

Epoch: "The Splinter," "Woodland Interior," "The Covert," "Tenants Harbor," and "Violence."
The Hudson Review: "On This Particular Morning."
The Quarterly Review of Literature: "Ghosts," "Hunting," "This Evening," and "The Night Calling."
Riverrun: "Shotgun."
The Yale Review: "Invocations (1), *An Elegy*," first printed as "Invocation, An Elegy."

"Pastoral Meditation" was printed in a limited edition under the title *An Eclogue: Pastoral Meditation* (Angelfish Press, 1971).

"Ghosts" and "On This Particular Morning" were republished in The Borestone Mountain Awards *Best Poems of 1970*; "Invocations (1), *An Elegy*" was republished in The Borestone Mountain Awards *Best Poems of 1971*.

21660

ITHACA HOUSE
108 N. PLAIN STREET
ITHACA, N.Y., 14850

For Fran, my wife

Taking Up the Serpent

CONTENTS

INVOCATIONS

1 An Elegy

All I have of Doc Gaye, who set my poisoned right
Foot right, is a crosscut scar he gave me when I
Was fourteen. But he begins to come more and more
True, bleacheyed and somehow sinuous, with time
And luck. Now, if I think of a gutshot buck
Bedding down in its last night on earth, or of
A cartorn coon stretched moonstricken, kicking,
Where the dead sicken with the taste of mine dust
In the burntout south of Missouri, it is only to find
Him once more in the eye

Of a boy falling, fallen into fangdriven sleep.
It is to make him come clear, here, at least,
As that lonelyliving partaker of private fury
Who mysteriously lost his wife many years before
I found the wrong path in an orchard, and began to walk
With more than I'd bargained for. Gone perhaps
Are the rent limbs of soldiers he patched and tucked
In place, as a surgeon in two world wars: gone
As the eloquent fog of rye, in my memory,
That was upon his breath:

(Or the field where I tunneled through honeysuckle
Near the still roil of a greensnake
Among still blossoms, in an aura of sweetness that takes
The breath away: where I hobbled my imaginary bay
In the sure eye of the lizard, quick
In the sun, never thinking of Doctor Gaye)
—But the dowager owner of over half the town?
Will she ever forget that incurable pinch like a bite,
In this life or any other, in the drugstore next
To his office, time and again?

1

Watching him lurch at you on the sidewalk, he
Could be like anything you'll dream of meeting
On the wrong path; and in foulsmelling tweeds,
As pebblysplotched as the skin of a diamondback,
Looking lithe as a sprinter, he pulled his car one day
Onto a wooded lane while making a house call,
Turned off the ignition, lay down, and died of a heart
Attack. He cut me back to life. Now I
Must go: back into cherishable lies, into the bad
Performance of my youth,—

Into the eyebewitching chiaroscuro of timber.
I must take certain paths again, with a foot changed
Forever. I will follow old ways to God knows where
They disappear: beside a barn unused since the 'thirties,
A ramshackle outdoor privy, or a smokeshed
Near a weathered clapboard house, where black-
berries grow in the windows of the parlor: where
In the chinks of the fireplace, the rattlesnake
Composes his fury: waiting: accursed, accumbent,
Coiled round the dark of his eyes.

2 *Supper; induction*

As if *Once* were
                    A time when quail and woodcock fell
        Laden with shot among briars
And came forth as
Redolent gold
                    To be eaten with gladness and prayer
Where the wild pecansavor
Of turkey
                    Was shared with praise and thanksgiving, may
My speech come hot as a banquet
And serve as a source of renewal

2

Vinegarlaced, and sustaining;
              For I have taken
       The woodsroad that meanders
Away from the common storms
Toward Celeuthea,
                        Wanders sinuous
                      As the pinegrain
          In slain trees of an abandoned room
              But darker, through clerestorylit greengloam,
       Archaic untenanted shade

              Where the deathriddle lays
                Mossfurred, bleachboned, its curious

              Testimonies away from the sun;

I shall wander much
I shall stay a long time in these coverts,
In this covertmaking wilderness

Making hymns I shall weep and laugh
       And mumble,
And being unchary of sorrow laughter
And darkness
       I shall praise;
              I shall study the naming of others, burdock
                        Fernsori, nuthatch, the gladevole
                          Gracing the nest of the sparrowhawk,
              The furtive woodduck,
              The stumpbourned clutch of the great horned owls,
       The clickerbeetling grasshoppers taking wing
              Away from my path;
I shall rest,
       Sitting quietly often, hoping
              For the place of grace, for
              The long silent swoop away from the self,
                        The reverse of the high hawk's stoop

From the quotidian curlicues of his screeing
in thermals;
I shall watch the whitetail buck's
Willowy browsing in the stillness of his beddingbrake
And make up hymns in praise of his being
There saying

You resemble in headgear and color
The tree and its ensemble here
Where willow and rock know how
To be silent with Thee;

It is good to have seen Thee;
For in time even the best things
Take on a worthlessness
Without those who represent them—

And I shall make ditties
Of haruspication according
To the clefs of the woodgrain
Found in the blowdowns, and by
These sinuous auguries
Make light
Of the dark that looking
Into blooms
Toward the manifest;

I would come upon overgrown loggingroads
In the hills from which the oak and pine,
The greatgrowing epical lumber of the past was skidded,
And rejoice at the ease of passage that
These ways into forgotten umbrage allow,
And I shall give myself to abandonment
For the nightly Visitor is at the window of the impenitent,
While I sing a song of my own composing;

I shall study the cleistogamy of the pansy, and hope to
emulate it;
I shall whisper psalms into the fastnesses of the snail,

                    The cloverforested mossbanks at
                    The foothills of the fallen
                    Redcedar's soilclung
                    Rootpinnacles;—
                              I have looked to the highground valleys
                              I may never wander in the wintry meadows of
And looking up thought on
     How there are no old mountain climbers
     Noted for derring-do;
     And so
              Have beheld
              The erableached ridgegrade crosshatching
Of rockslid timber
         A golden
Eagle's spiral above the river-
                         slow swirls
                         Of decelerating
Current wherein the manmade logjam grinds,
And have latched my desirous vision on
         Swiggles of snow down basaltlofts fused by orogeny;
         And sorrowing have sung
There are still signs of motility higher than ours
Will take us
With any ease,
              Or lacking
              The strength of grace
                 At all,
                    At all; . . .

So that
There are days such as these when I come down
Toward twilight
     With the eldereyes of hillslope oaks upon me,
     Away from the dreamed haven of Ygdrasil
     The Great Ash Tree,
         When I
Make an issuance out of jackpine,

And approach
                A vaporghostly house,
        Where copperheads coo to their young
        In the cool of an overturned washbench,
                And the crest of the basewormed gatepost I pass by
                        Ruffles its hackles, whirrooing off toward the dark;

Let the table be laid with a cloth in the heat of remembrance;
        The night
                        Nigh
                Falling be bodied, heavy
                With summer; presage of
                Dark
                Be dark
                    As the dark
            Of this calling;
The larkyielded stumped fields sing out
            Of breezewaft richened by onion,
            Sweetened by sweetcorn and
                    Sumac, pokeweed
        And lilac,

Let the whole thing strongly
Begin, from where I am:
                                        These words

This food
Be seasoned by river
        Fog fingering pine, by river fog swaying aroma
                A long ways over these meadows,
                The swarmed cow's moony
        Putrescence and
The lightningstruck horse's mouth
                Grinning a tale of deliverance;
May these words gather scent from the river,
        From Black River moonveiled with light;
        From lowdown cedar
        And the locust tree

On fire with the smell of wild honey
May this wordmeat garner a tang:—

Where the crosscut saw's
Harp hangs
Still
On the knoteyed wall,
The handrough planking
Returned to the spider's dominion and
In summer to seignory
Of the copperhead and the bee,

I would set to a meal not found
By diligent seeking;
Where the backyard kettle's waxed green
Amid honeysuckle,
And the rustscabbed roofing creaks
Praise of a rich desolation;
Where the homegrown graveslabs whisper
Their verse on faith and forbearance
I have come to a lintel
Awry, and enter
Therein:
I break the bread of the curve of all my days.

GHOSTS

... ruined, futile writing and unkillable defiance
—James Agee, *The Morning Watch*

Now the codger caretaker sleeps in the cemetery.
Dead to the world
                              in the window of his hut
An empty jar of moonshine
Glows like the eye of a bobcat caught in headlights,
And what rises or falls now
                              wildly
Accepts the power of simple expression that has been
From the beginning: it is time for aging
Lovers to close their doors, windows, their curtains
Lock themselves together in the dark, and fly anywhere
Out of the harnessed land

On the wings of their nightmarish arms.
It is in this light, in which all forms are gigantic
And small enough to crawl in the marrow of bone,
That the snakes we killed in youth, hacked
To pieces with shovels, with scythes, chopped
In two with powerful mowers, flattened in shorn hayfields
Under tractor tires, or bruised with pitchfork tines
In the mellow gloom of barns,
                              stuck on the points
Of wooden Arthurian swords, and displayed for the anguish
Of mothers, through screened-in back porches
                                        stir again

Again, and more than they did when alive.
Now something strangely sinuous may pass through the wall
Of timber
                move as naturally as the god of all
Things primitive into the vaporous lowlands, and tailstand

On junked cars in the moon's white light.
In a yard where children dream in their tarpaulin wigwam,
A luminous kingsnake drifts out of honeysuckle, out of sweet-
smelling vines

                          and coils the handlebars of an unhoused tricycle:
On logging roads, on back-country county roads,
On the wellworn paths that cattle take to a thousand ponds

Copper heads are searching now for the whites of their bellies,
For the separate riven skins
That rise out of dust in the shapes they took when they died;
And on hillsides where men walk in darkness at noon
Ever conscious of Adam and Eden's
Thorn in the heel

                          the fungus of ancient timber
Moves: cracks: gives way,
As diamond backs rear up, up-

                                        curl from the grave-
groping place like tongues, terrific as vampires
On the drive-in movie screen in the valley below—rear up

And fly with the grace of unknown beasts
To beat their wedgeheads on windows battened against them,
To crawl in ghostly skins, in leafy draintroughs
Of houses they never saw in their wicked, hidden lives—
Feeling for holes in the flesh
Of human dwellings

                          for any way to get in, GET IN
In before dawn, before they crinkle like dust on a well-
house floor, in the cluttered corners of garages,
On staves in a kitchen woodbox beside the door,—
GET IN

                 among the warm, the tremendous bare feet

They struck at mostly in vain, in their old sluggish days.

SITTING AT HOME

Sitting at home,
 Beyond all fingers of ridge that point
At any time into the past, I will stand up suddenly
 Out of the changeable sun-and-woodshadow dappling
Of my hunting cap, quick as a jumped buck's scut
 And shoot, in the motion of rising,
At a fox squirrel's
 Brilliant pellmell locution in leaffire above me. . . .
Somewhere a bass breaks water to spit a hook out

In a twinkling, then is gone; and I am back, near the floor
 Of this hillside, watching the small pieces of hickory
Float to noiseless earth
 Seconds after
This game should have ended. It is now, for the first time
 Since just before dawn, I know by a change of shade
On the rim of one eye—my father is near where I move
 In woods. We have found each other by slowly hunting
Apart, on the track of the circle

We began to create
 At one point in the dark: going, gliding each his own way
Back to back, across the unknowable sleep of snakes
 That neither of us had ever wished to imagine
The other discovering, frightfully, underfoot;
 Till we turned into light,
Still hunting
 Shoulder to shoulder, where the hillflown spangling of dawn
Ruddied the ghostsun web of forest between us.

Thus we have moved in accord all morning, halting
 To translate the quiet shots of our separate hollows
Into game; and have come
 At length to this

Unforeknown place, where acorn cuttings burn darkly
    In the midday pattern of sun upon them, and where,
As our eyes concoct a sign for this drawing-together,
    Something whispers, rustles high-up, and the body falls
Down, striking sharply at our feet.

THE SPLINTER

There are deaths we would all do anything to avoid:
Far away, almost out of time, in time out of mind
For the most part, in odd moments of our darker selves;

So that, perhaps after spraying a wasp some afternoon,
After making a wasp dance like blazes in July
In a puddle of Real Kill on the window sill—

After watching the red splinter of his stinger shoot
Wildly in and out, in and out of the hell
Of his body, . . . one of us

Might run that night, into a field, years back,
To where a burned-out, smouldering shanty still sizzles,
Pointing every-which-way in its fire-hose pool of water,

And help lift the mannequin body of a man
Out of ashes, going to pieces, before waking up. . . .
For a long time, many years, we will live with such things:

With anything unbelievable, known without doubt,
That works in the body of thought like a sliver of wood,
Till an undeniable festering forms around it,

And all vision goes awry, like a plane in a storm.
When I was fifteen, I walked into woods as a man
Who was part of a search party. Three soldiers had blown

Away from their plane, with its wings; had come down
On a mountain in Missouri. One of them sticks
In remembrance, wholly still. He is not the one

That fell incredibly straight, not disturbing a leaf,
Into a rocky glade, and stood on his head
In the sun till he melted into a puddle; nor

Is he the one that left the impression of something
On a road, and broke like a gourd in blackberries
Yards away. But may the image recede, the furrows

Set in the nodded head of the last, kingly one,
Who eluded us for days, at his place in the air,
Disappear, and not cast me again, as the statue

Of a boy looking up, under the burnt pine-spear
Of the tree on which he sits, the splinter-end
Growing out of his back at the neck, his legs sticking out

Wildly askew, away from the wood of his trunk,
Like those of a woman photographed making love.
Any fire-tempered sapling may become that one;

As he became, in a trice, awesome as myth,
A man with a tree for his body; and without warning
At night, at the edge of a far field, sunlit, with cattle

Grazing in the foreground, where a boy in overalls
Is trotting behind a german shepherd, shouting
Silently, waving a stick — suddenly . . . he is . . . there.

HUNTING

Much as if I should look once more
At the photograph of father dressed up for his world war,
Wearing his flight jacket:
And by a burst of flame
Come true in the back of the mind,
Be somewhere over North Africa
Under his B-17 in the ball of a turret:
More times than once I have raised
My head in timber, alone,
To the afterlight of the sun,

And find myself as one
Lifting the rusted wireloop from the gatepost
Of a graveyard lost in woods.
I have left my aging father's brand-
spanking new trail bike standing
In a clearing, behind me.
What I feel now and then
As I pass through the gate of this fence
And sidestep the briared and brambled
Dust of these thoroughly washed in the blood of the lamb,

Is only an upcoming breeze, that moves
Not these, not these;
But riffles the whole hillside
To place its strange hand in my hair.
This is nothing beside the shock
Of a wedge head striking one's foot
By this sunken grave or that,
Where thorns long since took root
Within the breast of one
Who fell at Bloody Angle, or rode with Sheridan;—

Or of starting
As out of a dream, to see a hunting coat
Rise, from behind a headstone,—
Take the form, out of evening mist,
Of one's own veteran image
Paces away.
I have met my father.
We do not look at each other
For anything like a moment,
Then tally the dead on our hands

Walking out of the overgrown graveyard;
Shut the gate with its noose of wire,
And ride the trail bike
Double, back to the car.
I balance our rifles between us,
My knees at my father's hips, our game in his blood-
lined hunting coat
Which I wear for the length of the ride,
With the stiff foreleg of a squirrel rubbing my back
All the way. When the bike is secured in its rack,

Where it shines
In despite of dust, like something indelible,
Like the only hope of renewal for aging hunters,
We go down to a stream aglide in the mist of its alders,
And kneel, beside the fastrunning water.
Here we gutout the game, saying
This one you got, that one's mine.
We talk as successful hunters will,
With wellearned, dead flesh between us,
And some sense as to where we are, turning home after dark.

CYCLING SEAWARD

On the second day of June
We pedal together, alone:
Myself, and my wife of one day,
Toward something we cannot see,
Having sought the full honeycomb
Of whatever we have become,

And drunk with milk of the wine-
laced devil-may-care of love.
The motion we make as we move
By means of our feet is a sign
Of anything freely given
On earth: as it is in heaven

We float toward the sandrind of land. . . .
Something starts, in the back of my mind.
Now as if I should stop, and stand
In the light of this sunless dawn
On the rise we begin to descend:
Drink from my flask, like one

Who has hefted a whaler's harpoon,
And discovered on still seafields
The large movement of something unknown:
I am waking a shape like a child's,
A form that will not come forth,
Or may come in a mist over water

As the ghost of a son or a daughter.
We are somewhat short of the shore. . . .
I think of a song to dispel
The ageold tremor I feel
As we cycle apart, with one will,
Myself, and my wife of one day,

Toward the near caterwauling of gulls:
"This is the happening earth
Where the fig tree puts forth her green."
Thus, whisperingly, I proclaim
In the teeth of the sea's own voice.
"I have gathered my myrrh with my spice:

I am my beloved's, she is mine."

SHOTGUN

It was my father's call
Up the stairs
As if he were waking me to go hunting,
Beckoning me to come from the heights
Of childsleep
down
through the cloud-
driftseeming oily aether of bacon,
Into the gloom of the kitchen,
Where the leaves outside the tablewindow
Were not yet furred with sun:
It was that call to me
as back
Into a world where I never broke my neck,
But where
once I swayed
With the topmost
Halfsustaining boughs of a tall pine
Tree, and two or three times tumbled
Almost down
and out
Of the sky,
To where the spirits
Of flayed squirrels had made to my knowing
Their roundsong ratchetsound
Over the woodglades,
In the feetspattering twilight of the high timber,
Where often I had heard
In the meeting hollow
the strung game
Whisper vengeance at the nightfalling:
It was that call to me
That told me first
How Death held fast in grip my father's father.

Now I, my father's father's singer
These years later,
            Know there was no wind-
        struck music at his leaving
                                his stroked
Head wholly agape and ruined jaw straining
                From the low angling of the roof
        Toward the window framing
The woodpile
                        and the cradling bend of bucklegs
        Holding
                    in a sickroom's-sunroiled-
            Sundayschool-picture's lance
        Of elegaic dust
                            the five-years-unfired
Doublebarreled twenty-gauge.

THE UN-NAILING OF HAWKS

An Easter Service

Rise God, judge Thou
The earth in might
they sing,
And Hell is well-nigh vanquished
In the manifold unfolding of this season,
Of Immanuel Our King Lord God Hosanna . . . .

—And I am shuffling
Down a heat-floating back country road
Back into my boyhood toward
A fence I found deep in Missouri
and begin
To tuft it with larkspur, flyblown and wild

Flowering clematis,
Of untended post and barbed wire.
Should the breeze alter now in my hair
I may find some ragged thing spanning a field-gate,
With four foot
of spread wing attached.

It might, as it was,
Be a goshawk, its eyes
No longer on fire near
The calm source of killing, hanging
here:
Or a redtail's head aswarm with the meaning of sunlight,

Taking shape in my brain
In a halo of horseflies and dustmotes
That I try to create

with a vengeance:
It could be anything too wild for its own good,
About to die out: the kestrel, the marsh-haunting

Harrier
the rough-
legged, the broadwinged hawk:
The Everglade kite or the Merlin,
The osprey, the sharp-shinned hawk: it could well be any
Such feather-pelt, bloated and working with maggots, but

I would not have it
So: for *Death cannot keep*
His prey

they sing, where the doe's
Still fresh hide strains from the side of the henhouse,
Strains now to learn what god has a new way

Of being in this land
Where the mule dies beaten bloody
In the furrow rather than budge,
Where a loud idiot sorrow

is wrung from peas
And meal, till Christ is King:

Lord God of Poachers at the end of the dwindling
Branch road
And their quartz-eyed wives,
Unspike my blood of pity,
Let me rave:

Let it begin
With the harpy eagle's head,
A million years ablaze on the tines of the crest,
Till, harpy-sized
In the smoky flawing of spring,
With more dare than a creature has owned
Since the first curdled sun danced

                                    forth

And stood on a hill
As a god sprouting every-which-way,

                                    it should rise
Up out of the day-
broken glitter of meadows, like what one will fight
Out of linen

As from the grave
To escape at night,
And find anyhow on the curtains, with moonlight wan
Through one wing.
When this thing is surely arisen
For backwoods assemblies of god

                                    heads will be turn-
ing to wonder a moment before such looming over a pasture
Of something

                                    something
Darkening — dark enough for the folk
Guitar: men in all
Walks of cattle will become stockstill, will drop their shotguns
Like milkpails,

Will put down the nails
In the scars of their hands
When this thing comes to pass

                                    comes to show
The wrenched and the hunched

Their strangest reasons for praising the Lord,
For raising holy hell in the wilderness:
                                        it will come
Bearing miles of powerline over crinkled-up forestry towers,
Ripping the quilting of fields
Apart, with its scream: proclaiming
By talon and wing-beat
That the Lion fall down with the Lamb, yea, that all streams flow as red
As the Hebrus,

For the Word become Flesh, at last.

ON THIS PARTICULAR MORNING

I hear bravuras of birds....
                                    —Walt Whitman

1

Last night: March rain
Splatting, spits of brightness, thunder; the hills
Fillingup like barrels with water
                                    runnels failing
To hold their own,—now this: I dress and pass out
Through my door into light.
                                    And the world is dowered by birds
On this particular morning, in this vaporous quiet
The red-bellied woodpeckers come to the feeders in pairs;
And the robins, those firstlings
Of spring wrangle toward me
                                    singing: warbling more good-
naturedly than musically moving out
                                    down from the oak
Trees up along the ridge.
                                    Now the chickadee brings
Its three-note melody, and the white-breasted nut-
hatch trills as if
To the bewick riding upside-down on the suet feeder,
Swinging with it
                                    adding his mating call to the crazing
Grace of this quiet chorus,
                                    to the strophe, here!
And antistrophe out along the multiflora hedge,
Where white-crown and white-throat sparrows skirr and whirr,
Where meadowlarks, now
And again!
                                    take to the air with the flair of angelic
Quail.

2

                —In this loud stillness of the sun's slow
Rising
                now like my long self's others, I
Would wingedly rise
Up wholly out of *it*
                      out of scythe-snath sickle
Whiffletree and clevis,
As my heart goes out to these like my whole self:
As, overhead
The skein of Canada geese, that squall of honkers
Passing to some fake refuge in the far North,
Receives unknowingly my utmost blessing.
My desire in this particular light is the lost,
The forfeited grace of birds
                  the incredibly clear
Call of the cardinal this morning, the unkillable strength
Of white-throat sparrows that in a week will journey
To the edge of the Arctic tundra.
                  I would be, BE
By God with them, all of them,
                  I think: or riding
The topmost limb of a timberline wind-gnarled pine,
In the dwelling-place of the last surviving buteos:—
Learning the stormy elan of these jays
                  that are coming
Into focus like memory, like hell or high water,
Terrible as blood-
shed in the corner of my cornfield, coming out of nowhere
To strike there!
            and there!

And more,
           more than anyone could handle in this life,—
Where they rip the stuffing out of the light-blinded owl.

THIS EVENING

This evening, at first, we did not see deer:
My wife and I driving into the countryside
Craning our necks, looking into

And as though through the mist hanging in the swales, —
Suspending upon alfalfa
The numinous night-waking dream

Of the screechowl and whippoorwill,
Or rising along the timber-swirls of the creeks:
Like the ghosts of deer, maybe,

Or the spirits of less romantic-looking creatures:
Of woodchucks shot by farm boys
And left to rot in July,

Or those killed by sportsmen with telescoped rifles
From great distances, blown
To bits by high-powered ammunition, or

With only their heads shot
Off, and the rest of the carcass carefully stuffed
Down the animal's burrow;

Of field mice scattered by hawks over the barn lot,
And of small birds, unsensational retiring birds —
Waxwings, forest sparrows, wrens —

Caught by the shrike
And pinned, still alive, to a barb of wire on a fence,
With the underside bared for the beak, the pike-like strike.

TENANTS HARBOR

Thou shalt have the whole land for thy park and manor,
the sea for thy bath and navigation, without tax and
without envy; the woods and the rivers thou shalt own,
and thou shalt possess that wherein others are only
tenants and boarders.

　　　　　　　　　　　　　　　—R. W. Emerson, *The Poet*

1

From where I am
Perched on a cabin porch
I look out upon a cove,
Where herring-gulls veer between me
And celebrant islets full
Of processional main-mast firs,

As the sun tilts to its best height,
Leaving brightness all over offshore:
There, birds mew louder and louder
As if to counterpoint twilight,
Though it's midday still where they are,
And nearly full dark here.

The tide-wash conches the ear.
The mind slips out of the self
As if into swells flecked with whitecaps,
Where the useless oar jolts in the oarlock,
Making no headway through water;
And the idiot prow lurches off

The appointed path, swinging
Back the way one has come
Through terrors of effort before,
Destroying what strength would be taken
In writhing to turn, turn back, back
The monotonous churn of the sea:—

So I have been caught and swirled
By the wing-glinting magic of otherhood;
Have suffered the undertow
Of the self's unbeckoning cheepers;
Have heard both hiss and bird-rasp
A-lurk in the drowned bone's stark

Whorl of the sea-held granite
That proffers nothing to me
But what I find in the clam-hod
After the clams are eaten
By the bloated raccoon in its tree:
The fish smell, the absence of god.

2

But in this landscape where nothing is fixed,
This country of islands and coves, sea-iris and white sea-roses,
Where not even the mammoth shore boulders stay in one place,
There are beasts to bring one round to one's best side
As into a bay of calm water, surface-quiescent,
Where one pulls the skiff through tide-abandoned kelp,
Then, for a yard or two, over loaf-sized rocks
And the pine-prickly backs of sand-dollars,
To half-hitch the mud-caulked cord round a hardwood sapling,
On a windless escarpment of bay, a moorspot of willowy stillness,
Where the gulls waddle in time
To the out-going sea's rallentando,
Amid bleached sticks, shards of clamshell, snail-wrack and
                                                  seaweed-wisp:
A place lightly sloshed by wavelets, of deer trails worn through
                                                      the grass,
And of silence:
Till

Just inside the firline,

A lone raven bursts from the dappling of a thicket,
Jawing rachetey, the wings aren't clear of briar, yawing,
A lot of flapping, a
Wallop, then
Swish

And free in the air, casting
Out toward a safer region of the North Atlantic, sounding
The depths of deliverance among thermals, clear,
Clear, in sea air.—

And I think of the ospreys we saw the other day, my wife and I,
When we went to the harbor-side quarry
Abandoned even by Finns,
And stood amid broken-jaw chunkings
Beside the alewive-less waters:
Watching the ospreys
Hover the bristling nest, a thing too large for just birds, hover
Till I advanced
On the guyed pole the rath is atop of,
The useless hauls of the quarryworks looped in their rust,
Watching one wary osprey, the male, a-tilt on a guywire: then
From out the thing
Came a schriee
Schriee
                    and the female, darker and larger, lifts
Off the hodge-podge of driftwood and shore rubble,
A shadowy motion
                              like a well
Forgotten dream of retribution
Sliding out
                    into the windcurrent,
Fighting the air-tide in order to get above me,
The white undersides of the primaries splayed like a cry,
Telling how I will know
The spirit's serried others
                                        the farfetched grace of the raven

Round headlands dusky with light: the arete of the osprey
Now
        far off, in flight.

3

Sky and water: the same dark blue through darker leaves;
And the blackducks bank, tack, and dive
In breaking scores
Away from the hacked sabre of the harbor, out
Over the mud-shimmering tidal flats, their veering
Tuned to the quaank   *quaank*
Of their diminishing.
The be-islanded waters, calm till now, grow
Still.

I consider the leavings, in this large-scaped watery land,
The sodden gulls I may never call from the slip.
It is time
To quit.

Tenants Harbor, Maine
Summer, 1970

WOODLAND INTERIOR

I rejoice that there are beasts:
The raccoon that skulks from the hill at twilight, waddling
Stealthily, stop
And go, in
And out among deadfall pine, those trees
Bedecked with slugs, fatmaggoty yellow
Or orangish-red earth leeches,
Has no fear of me, none at all: would do me in
Eschewing my garbage can
If he were three
Or four feet longer:
I have held a sick chickadee
Warm in my hand, a feathery pup, and matter
For some rejoicing,
But I have also
Dreamed the business of birds,
The eyes pecked from the gartersnake in the rosebush,
Crows swarming the lame rabbit, augering the eyes,
Gulls, carefully extracting flesh from the living sandcrab:
These are common
Occasions, in the land of the utterly free.

I rejoice that there are beasts,
Though they are of little importance to me
In their beastly, torn
Going: they are of little importance to me
Though I have inspected with care
The bloated woodchuck cornered too far from its lair,
                                        belly-up, sodden,
Quite sodden, purple skin under the fur, the anus protruding,
Left shoulder broken,
But the other three hands in the air,

A skyward rigorous clutching,
The tightfisted varmit,
Of no importance to me.

Where the woodspinner gathers the whole of the dawn
On the great far side of the marble of his body,
There now I make my study, for I have been there, on both sides:
I have walked through the dark of morning,
Toward its first, heartcalming light,
Uphill and down, deep down,
To sit beneath this tree:
I give my back slowly to bark:
I assume the poised slouch of one hunting:
I watch for the changes wrought
On the nearby hardwoods, of morning:
This could be more or less
Than the blackest place of receiving, I think, not knowing my
                                                        thought;
But the kingsnake sways from the jays' nest, out of the shearedoff
                                                        pine,
And the hawk plays out into thermals, fletching the dawn with its
                                                        cry:
The web of the wood takes light, bit by bit waking brightly,
The filaments beaded with wet. I am motionless, eyeing the small.
My gut is a tangle achurn,
Achurn with the need of repairing.
My eight legs dance toward the fly, the fly,
The only beast of consequence I see.

PASTORAL MEDITATION

In Memory of Theodore Roethke

1

Thou, invoker of Whitman, over the treetops I float thee a song,
Over the winddappling on the glazed breast of the Quinault River:
Over the violetblooming prunella, in the gloom of an Olympic summer,
Over the spearing loft of the hemlocks at all seasons,
Over the hidden vine maple, saffron in autumn,
And into the world of the slug emerging from its black sheath,
To thee, I float this song:
And over the blue deathclarity of the high glades,
In the quiescent garbage beyond the rictus of the suburbs,
Under the wintering gutter's drip
I would have this heard—

This maundering plainsong taken up in the spring,
Uttered beyond the chicanery of dabblers,
The chinoiserie of those with adequate talent—
By the wholly
Dumb, and the innocent:
Where the hermit thrush warbles toward silence,
Birdshy, hidden.

2

We came upon a river, nearly as large
As the Seine at Paris, in the evening toward sunset,
A river which the prairie grass had hidden.

Alone, in the canoe
We come back, and go
Down a branch of the Saginaw,
The sky without a cloud,
The atmosphere pure
And still.

The wilderness was before us,—
A gorgeous dwelling,
A living palace for man,
Though as yet the owner had not taken possession.
All quiet and serene.
Our voices became fewer,
Sank to a whisper;
Until, by the influence of this scene—
Wrote Tocqueville in July, 1831—
We lapsed into a peaceful reverie . . .

All the remembering eye perceives
Partakes of the special Death-in-Life of summer—
The speckled lash in the crevice of the ledge,
The dazzling august fields of Queen-Anne's-lace,
The wing-flash of the redwinged blackbird among cattails,
A momentary scarlet, a blur through reeds,
And the catbirds behind the henhouse rasping out of time.
Is there a weightier music in the memory?—than the bluejays rangling
With starlings in the persimmon grove at dawn,
Or the hawk's upward-drifting cry,
Its tail flared with a glow the color of sassafras;
The meadowlark's arc-pitching twitter cut over the field path,
Or the silence curdling the evening
After the crows have flown—?

I tend to my own melody of existence,

To certain resurgencies,
I call on what I know to make this song:
The distances fallow with furze,
Along the watery reaches,
The quietness ways, where tadpoles flicker like minnows
In time to my passing shadow,
And the waterspiders browse the pale-green scum of the creekpools,—
Where bullfrogs, the twilight croakers, are warier at noon,
Backing silently into the nesses of the watercress,

Ruffling the silt of the stream-bottom, their backs like verdigris,
Merging the submerged root and the mossed stone.

3

Is it time for the owl's flight?
I hear the meowing of a cat under my window.
Spring's not here;
But sun flanges the dawn-shadowy east sides of buildings.
There'll be no god-luring for me today. No Blake-thing hill-hopping.
No fury of periodicity. Not even a lone marsh wren bubbling from
                                                        weeds.

In the evening, when the spunk's gone out of even the bearable Average,
The collective mediocrity of hours,
I have looked to the windings and yearnings of my ways;
Have wormed toward the undulant: the patterning
And re-patterning of the rattler's
Glide into the amber and auburn
Turning of fall,—
Toward the giant
Gar, scirrhoidal,
Waiting in the black of a flooded stump for swimmers.
Sing? I tend the dead. And hear, sometimes,
The gargle of an old man's going.
I've watched him beckon, crying, more times than once:
I see him now, a mote in the mind's eye,
Gun-rust gathering the worst of his sick-room's dust,
Waiting for light to fail on the wall calendar—
The one with the planting and harvesting days, the phases of the moon,
The birth-times of the grandchildren marked in pencil,
And the changeless abandon of a bird dog bounding through grass.

Now nothing rocks there, not wind in the rocking-chair,
Not even a ghost foot pumps the sewing-machine treadle.

The walnuts darken. The fall's the season. A time, poet,
For asters and chrysanthemums:—

But I smell the odor of rotting shad,
Their gullets ripped out by fish hooks,
Along the summery banks of the Mississippi.

4

It is winter.
The noise we make is nothing to the spheres.
Northward, the deer are dying.
At nightfall they wobble out of the coverts,
As dull with hunger as the survivors of Belsen,
And cross the iced ponds be-meadowed with snow;
A wary, straggling trek beneath the moon;
They bow their heads to the frosted dream of hay,
Among the cows in the barn lot.
Occasionally one of them is killed,—
Pulled down by dogs, running a broken field, or
Escaped from the slathering hamstrung dying,
Pulped by a tractor-trailor truck on the super-highway.

It is winter.
Think of the time when the last Irish stag was brought to bay,
A loop of drawn
Gut violet in the twilight,—
Pawing the spruce tangle,
Making ready to die.
In this time of annulled soothsaying,
Praise the underground electrical circuits in the suburbs,
The ten telephones in the ten-room house,
The refrigerator's hum,
The paraldehyde nailing the walls of the night together.

It is winter.
Lord,
I've had my nose to the ground;
But never under.

5

As the ghost owl wakes, stirs
Toward the last of twilight, wakes,
In the mast-hoard of duck bones, in ancient morsels of snake,
And fares
Forth, the visible
Spirit of an old silence,
A Death aglide through the crystalline snow-blue of conifers,
I let the mind go
Out, hunting over the roof-tops
As over the netherward black of hemlocks,
Preying upon These States.
For the sympathetic heart is broken; we stink in each other's nostrils.
As the talon strikes to the weasel's brain
I enter the nightmares of writhers in the diminishing small towns,
And the skulls of the living dead, in the amniotic slime-air of the
                                                            cities,
And find in the grotto-mouths below the cortex,
The watery-eyed purveyors of bug-spray and napalm.
I let the mind go out,
For the swan is gone, but the stench of the swan abides:
I perch at a field's edge, in the dark of buckbrush and oak:
I see, in the near distance, the smear of the mid-country cities,
Hear the hosts cry hosanna in the hamlets of Iowa,
In the jerk-water towns where the first-born are mostly albinos:
Where His Name like sweet perfume shall rise with every morning
                                                            sacrifice,
Where the brow that once was crowned with thorns is crowned with
                                                            glory now.

As the talon twists in the weasel's heart
I would enter the heart of this land:
I would enter the heart of the veteran asleep in Nebraska,
Where Ezra Pound shadow-boxes, in a prison-yard on the road to
                                                            Viareggio:
I would enter the heart of the prison guard in Arkansas,

37

Where the inmate dies on a table, choking in vomit,
With electrodes attached to his big toe and his penis:
I would enter the heart where the will to dig potatoes well
Is dessicated by the fulfilled promise of Money:
I would leave this land no fit habitation for the barren-ground caribou:
I would leave our cities smoking as they smoke now, but with less shame.
Yea, I call for fires in the City,
For a lively ruin to descend upon this country:
I would turn the charlatan's rhetoric to its best use:
To char the lovers a-bed,
To stuff the child back in the womb,
To dull the delicate ear in youth,
That it come not to its fore-doomed maturity,
That a man hear not in future years this screed, or the likeness of this
                                                                                    screed,
And lament that what was said in a lonely room
Taught no remnant to obey, instilled no loftier melody in thought,
Brought, as is the way with words, nothing to pass.

   6

We abide the season. We wait without reason
We wait
For what—?

The crescent of scoria-stain in the Mississippi,
Slag and sewage spreading among ice-chunks,
The sulfurous drift of the breeze,
Such signs as these,—
The bum's dangling
Sneeze beside the pier,
The dentist drill piercing the brain when the barge-cables strain.

Are the spindly fawns by the meadow-gate?
The high grasses swooning all one way on the hillside?

A weak doe feeds on sprout-growth in the river's cobbling.
Winter's ending.

7

Here. A prostrate log. Seedbed for cedar and spruce.
Nearby, liverworts, mosses, fern: fronds of licorice fern, let us say,
Yellow spathes of skunk cabbage: the primrose in the high-ground
                                                                          brakes,
And the April trilliums aching like girls to bloom:—
I call upon the Life-in-Death of spring,
When the beaver feed by twilight in the alder flats,
And spiders fatten in shafts of sunlight between wood-nymph and
                                                                          foamflower:
When the foxglove flowers, bell-flowering, purple and white,
And the hoof-print of the elk is brimed with snow-water.
Who attains knowledge of death, the sacred knowledge of death?
Ask the chickaree squirrel in a quarrel of providing,
The greensnake curling
Like an immortal scythe-snath from a limb;
The caterpillar in the white
Display of May,—

Or follow the melted snow to the coast
And the rotten gull, its flat side matted with sand,
Its eyes the ravin of ravens,
The wings crusted with salt.

8

Now I sit, at the close of this day, sit, and look forth:
In the recesses of cedar I see
The white tail-flicker of the junco's veer and glide,
And think of a lone merganser curvetting over the current of the Hoh,
Of a bald eagle's slow descent, black against the ice-blue of the sky,
Down from a sub-alpine stump on Mount Olympus.
I sit, with summer approaching,
With the wheat beyond the mountains
Straining from the umber shroud of fields,
And the new spring fragrant over the redcedars of the Kalaloch,
A world of maples draped with shags of clubmoss,

And elk herds grazing the wonder of the meadows.
With Death your Companion I watch you flee to the water,
Away from the ghostly pines on the hill,
Away from the upland glades,
The ferny loom of the trees,
And berries spuming the trunks of the Douglas-fir:
You glide, with Death your Companion,
Toward the beaver's den in the river meander,
Where the mimulus touch the streambanks with vivid yellow—
Where the light fails in the coastline hollows,
And the spray is flung like shekels over the offshore rocks:—

I leave you now,
Having done what I can do,
In the deepening exuberance of May,
In a plenitude of sounds composing silence:
I shake this plainsong's coverlet of mourning
From your encompassing One-singing multitudinous Self,—

I leave you the river's quiet mouthings to the steady slosh of the
                                                         tide,
And the seabirds quealing toward the lost
Dream of the mist.

THE COVERT

Having received permission from an askew-faced old lady to hunt
These woods, I arose in the doe-eyed hour before the morning
Star appears, abandoning the still dark flame of my wife,
And concocted a world less varied by fractures than sleep
As the god-fearing town splotched small

                                    smaller, then
Nothing at all, under the curve of the upland, there,
In the valley beneath me: till simple as loss, or flesh,
The high fields lay undulant with snow. I ascended these meadows,
As striding as knowledge through mist, unable to see
Much before me

             behind or anywhere
Else, but glancing all ways nonetheless, my feet chuffing deep
And deeper into the upland, till all of a woodlot's beetling
Of shade bristled for me, and I stepped to the softer snow

                                       in,
To the easy beguilement of trees:

                        I stood a moment:
The nothing around me grew restive: a snow-clump kicked loose
And plopped from fir-limb to stump, once, in the tree-gloom before

                                     me . . . .
When the snowshoed hare broke the retral buck-rack of deadfall
And left her fear deep as droppings in pad-prints behind me,
I came to myself, and hunted all day in that woodlot, the blood
From my writhen toes upward

                          growing more lovely, and cold,
Like the blood in a doe's gaped pelvis, the black basin
Of her pelisse, when she's hung on the meatpole to cure, in the last
Of October's fall, the recalcitrant fluid seeping, all night,
To her sex's socket

                   which, by the next dawn's merest ridge-brimming
Is poolsomely crystalled by rime: I hunted all day
In that timber, that metropolis crowded by absence, where the foot-
steps one has abandoned

                 sprout quick as cast stones in the dark

The companionless posit arearwards,
Sprout from the shuckings of acts and lives to slink benignly
Behind one, trying carefully not to smile: so I crossed
A far fence just at nightfall, with a sense of the unconfessable
Ice-ambered somewhere behind me; perhaps in the overturned Ford's
Bulking of snow-caulked embranglement, or in the dereglement
Of the mid-wood well's choked dark;
Or beneath the abandoned axehelve, the crock-shard snaggled with
                                                                          freeze,
Or the ledge-drippage thawing like spittle, where now and then one
                                                                    of us walks.

VIOLENCE

Dirge for Jackrabbits

1

It was a family outing for many
        Fathers showed sons how to swing
    The clubs while mothers and young
Daughters mostly stood by
        The sidelines spattered with
    Blood and watched
The drivers or brush beaters, who
        Had earlier loaded into
    Pickups and headed for
Strategic outposts on the perimeter of
        The driving area, drive or
    Beat: (some rapturous few of these taken
Tight by the slaughterheaded
        God slathering awake like
    A springloaded snake'stongue
Growth in the mind headed
        Straight for the trap at the end of the V-
    shaped fenced
Place, where the drive would
        Terminate):
    I could make
Other sounds against silence; here tell of remembrance
        Watertrickle underpurling sucklepurl,
    Or sing the escaped
Blurp of a crawdad scuttling under watercress
        In a creekbourne deep to a stillness,
    Could chirp of the hightailed and guileless or crow
To the careful profusions of woodswhirp whirping
        From the log of the chipmunk's chamber

Music on the outskirts of light;
But now I'm suffering the entourage enthrallment with meaty entwist
        To guttle my marrow
And harrow my waking, to put a fine briar to my sorrow here
Tonight:

   2

              Soon the entire area was surrounded by beaters,
        One every seventyfive to one hundred feet, and
When the word was given, all
              Started toward the point
        Of the V two miles away.—
Here much uncertainty lies
              Or crawls behind the eyes
        Grown rich with fright
Of a lot of jackrabbit, furtares (rabbits eat haystacks in winter)
              In the works of process, hopping mysteries that
        Do not know the mesne men of
Process, to keep alive, must always
              Challenge the unknown and
        Go as with a vengeance to
Where the most uncertainty lies
              Unversed in cul-de-sac, ambuscades, sorties,
        Brickbat and bat,—so that
Beauty when it is,
              As it rarely is,
        Found, shall have a touch of the marvelous, the unknown.—
So it is that where
              The circle of beaters got smaller,
        With horse riders and snowmobiles moving
Back and forth along the perimeter, back and forth
              And everyone shouting,
        Yelling and pummeling brush with his bat,
The timid rabbits within the ecraseur
              Were

Gradually forced toward the trap.
—We didn't see many at first and it
        Was hard to believe that
        Up to ten thousand were caught in the human net, but—
As when two years ago a week
           Before Christmas I climbed our streetful of snow
      To a delicatessen for beer,
And there the Greek proprietor said
         Look, and
      Pointed to where
A British TV show
         Displayed an African war, and four Nigerians held
      An Ibo wearing a breechclout, a young man
Standing between two soldiers, about
         To enter my life with a face I hope to forget, for
      Down on his luck like anyone
He tried to talk; to tell them he was looking for his wife and children:
         A highpitched plorative whine; but (and I, for one,
                         believed

      Him) they tied
His hands behind him then and
         Knocked him down; then the sergeant, whose jovial
      Blackguard lolling bespoke
What every 'man' below
         The Mason-Dixon Line would tag as 'nigger,' worked
      His Mauser's bolt and
Pulled the trigger—
         They were surely caught.

   3

      What is
The job for poetry
         In this season

                Of insufficient play, of
Act without honor or reason performed
                    Against the muddy
        Snow of everyday?—what
Is
                    The job
        For poetry?—
To carry such compost maundering to
                    Our beds
        Without delay?—
This is
                    No local problem, I would say:
        This is no failure of
Electricity:
                    No local failure of
        Electricity; but
A problem with the fine
                    Tuner of the heart's
        Complicity in error, I would say:
A problem with the fine tuner of morality:
                    Something's out of kilter, seems
        To me.—
This is no problem of the moon and stars, it seems to me:
                    This is no problem
        Settled
By complicated argument
                    I'd add: this
        Is no puzzlefoison for the reason, nothing to perform an act
Of muddlement upon—there
                    Is nothing
        For committee work in
This,
                    It seems to me:
There is nothing for the faculty
                    Of trapeze artistry in this, I'd say:
        Nothing for the foppery of thought.— This

Is beyond thought, and
          Far beyond all flurries of gentility; the garbage dump
    Of wise humility; the stumplegged comic
Prominent in our common
          Play, our act of life which is no life for
    You
Or me: this
          Is
    Beyond our present selves: we play a role for which
Redemption is a benison beyond the unknowable
          Lines
    Of thought of
The present play: speech
          Is the fog of the field's stricken reach
    That keeps us while we learn.

THE NIGHT CALLING

I look to my notebook for signs
Of what—more ancient than feldspar—
May divest

Itself of my brain. Like foxfire
Driftingly seen, IT
May float,

Moonslide over pine cones,
Curl through the boroughs of boughs,
And grow

Into life more simple
Than the goshawk straining to rouse from the blankness
Of paper,

Sustained, by my hand upon the thermals,
Or the great horned owl
Of his own

Accord has ever yet known.
So it is, I believe, for some
The soul

Finds its sooth motion
Gliding down, gliding
Down out of

Leafspilth, more sinuous than a bass,
From the nightgreen stage of becoming
Like a cottonmouth

Entering water.
                    Into that liquid being!
—A length of composed paroxysm,
Enclining

A sutured head
Down, toward the hypnotized ooze
Of the lilies,

An S-curving progress toward starlight.

GIVING CREDENCE TO THE CERTAIN

Certain old roads one gives a moment of credence to:
Ways of indescribable jolt in the fawn'slily drooping
Of twilight, when the day puckers like something turning
Its head, and the rusted brush
Hook abandons the pasture, curling
Through the fencewire it never encountered before,
And on out
                    into a world seeming bigger and bigger,
Till on the darkening asphalt the head
Arches up like the tip
Of a question asway
In the mouth of the onrushing chrome
                                        flickering
Seeking into the problem of light:

Then the cartire strikes with its groat'sworth of meaning
Inaugurating Ker-whoossh
                    and, in the long second
Of passover, the phlegm of gutspurt broiled to
The radiator, then the spinelinkage crackle and
Thwonk on the universal: then the rearaxle shadow
That no one has ever noticed, and then diminishing
Whine stretched on
                    on up the road.
That is one way of conceiving
It, the fatal surcease from tomorrow that few have
Desired: and, in the midday dark of the barn
Where heat is damp, and soft, like cobwebs caught with the face,
And the tobacco aroma of dung is heavy in straw,

Where the seat of the vanquished buggy is gnawn by rats,
And the snathes of the scythes swing kingsnakes down from the
                                                    rafters,

Near the dust of the chickenyard busy with "banty" roosters,
And the plumtree a boy protected from
The marauding catbird, lark, and jay
                                    hard by
The wellpump ashimmer as with fever and the choppingblock
                                                    encircled
By chickennumina dancing
Like cadences of the bedeviled and defiled,

                                        one sensed
How the Dragon may rear by the side of the road,
Smokey beyond lustration, bristling with exaltation,
A form etched blackly out of the misting of cherrybloom:
We go away from home, oh we go away from home,

It is in us to do it;
And in going from the place we must go from in order
Not to become the maggothost of the midsummer highway,
The twist of metal snared in the appletree
(A gift of the tornado that
Has lost itself to other shapes of wind),
The shot hawk nailed to the tarpaper siding of the henhouse,
Or the pinespear snagged into sky from the meadow of fescue—
By going from where we were
                                to where we will never be
Except in the mind
That attends
                    to the ropeswing swung from the luminous
                                                hickory tree,
To the dreamglistered bones of catbird, meadowlark, jay

Twinehung in the trophyroom outhouse: by going
So we accomodate ourselves
To a miraculous vacuity;
                            it is as if one were a spider
Travelling from one season to another, unravelling

From the dark bolus of the self the mode of going,
The high way slung between one unknown and another,
The lovely filamental gut aflow with shimmering in the early spring:
A sign of elemental progress, of waking
Into warmth, of dancing out of winter and
Into the loud threshing of the robin's wings, the studious beaks of
                                                              wrens,
And the enormous shade that falls
                              before the foot falls where
The "going from" incalculably ends.

WEST OF THE RIVER

I knew how it might be done: how to cut the skin away
From the hind feet, and separate the fatty tissue from the leg muscle,
Before guiding, gently, the hide
Down the length of the body toward the head, which
When the front legs were
                                        worked through the cape, could
Be severed, with one delicate circling slice
Of the wellhoned blade of my father's skinning knife:
And this is an art, such cleaning with care and no waste, not
Neatly mastered . . .

After the first time, when I had spilled her nutfilled moist
Mucous-sliding guts into an eddy,
And washed stray bits of viscera, bloodclot and shot
Out of her body, I stood in that evening's afterlight for a while,
Still in the yarrowy drift of wood and meadow,
Watching the bright parts floating away,
Away, pecked at by minnows:
                                        no more than a speck
At the last, a curious whiteness abob in the nightstain of shallows;
Then something snickered nearby, in moonfrothed willows,

And stars began coming flirtingly out of the water.
And I recall the time my father's father and I
Caught the broadwinged hawk:
                                        we were angling down
A ridge in late summer, the leafdrift copperhead's field day,
Trying to slide quietly along the hillside's steep incline
Through slippery underfooting of fernslime and root
When, like turkeys leaving the roost-tree
Or paired owls fleering away from the perch before full dawnlight,
A little behind us, overhead, near the spine of the hogback came

A rush, a feathery rush: I can still
See the glide above us of the two young hawks tilting
On unsure vanes between our attention
And the late afternoon sun, and the late afternoon
Sunsplintering the quills of their wings with russet

                                         surprised
By our passing into their hapless flight.
But one of them made it, splaying into the crotch of a downslope
                                     oak, hanging
On, in a fanfaronade of fluttering
Success: the other one struck the trunk halfway up and

Tumbled, a pound of hackles, to the ground: there
It hunkers, back to the trunk, wings halfspread for balance,
The hasp of the beak open, yellow eyes unblinking:
These things require a tendance and a modicum of praise;
Not for themselves alone but
For the radiance they raise like a nestling's hackles
Over the ridgebones and treecrestings of the mind;
Not for the jay's squall in the yard

                                but for the icy
Remembranced jay's squall lent

The dumbfoundering ramshackledom of Now:
As when a child one discovered under the buckthorn,
Or huddled against the bare dustdark under blackberry bush,
Or in a skeletal woods'edge blowdown
A nest of baby cottontails

                           (the parent rabbits absent—
Trapped in a gardener's boxtrap, maybe, or lost
To the spayed fat of a farmcat) and
Gathering the orphans out of the jampacked
Moment of discovery, brought them into the,

Hiddenly, dismayed hubbub of one's home,
Where mother was emboldened to make 'formula'—
Of handwarmed cow's milk and syrup—

54

And I worried the fluid into them out of an eyedropper,
Joyful at the delicate pink inside their ears,
The milkbeads fretting their troll-like whiskers,
And the hitherto alien warmth of their small lives:
So that it was difficult to sleep,

                                 and I woke
To the irritation as of peepfrogs throughout the night;

And, getting up early,
Before rime had wetted the rooster's comb,
Before anyone else was stirring,

                            went
Through the quieteerie house
To the warm corner of the kitchen
Where they had been tucked in, went,
To be rendered unextensive, caved-in,
Congealed: to find them
Flatlooking; clawing indelicately up the boxwall;

Unseemly rigorous attitudes;
Eyes less lively than marbles,
Too much white of the wrong side showing;   as when
A child one discovered
And out of discovery grieved, unchary of sorrow, a kind of
Jubilation giving of one's self
Grieving on the dark ground bordering the backyard garden,
Sorrowing down to a rhythmic calm, calm

                                   calm:
Turning with a spade the easyturning loam.

THE ABANDONED

Timber deepens more and more this glade
Far gone to brambles maybe sought by deer
In the January twilight of the year,
But this morning there is not one buck or doe.

Yet as a solitary place may not be lonely,
This lonely house is not quite solitary,
A smoky length of kingsnake lets me know.
(If there were some good reason for venturing

Through underbrush where a rusted innerspring
Might whiplash into copper-colored flesh,
Or dust sway out of the woodbox by the door,
I don't think I would mind so much the strain

Of studying leaves on this curled linoleum floor,
Before opening a chest, or an old crock.)
At any rate I won't be coming back,
For maybe another year or two or three:

Whether the razorstrap slithers away from its hook,
Hangs where it is through the whole century,
Or coils in a splotch of sunlight at the window
To watch me side-step the rotted axletree.

But the skeletons in the closet (I will believe)
Only suffer the mice of their eyes until I go.

A PLACE WHERE IT'S COLD

I make a place now where it's cold,
Where tenfoot icicles sawtooth
The eaves and gables of abandoned farmsteads
And the snow drifts
Unmarked into pines from the sinuous hillroads;
Where the wind whines through the weatherpocking of lost outbuildings,
Whines down from where roosting turkeys gland the snowspruce,
Tuning the waste of the lowlands to its own desolation
Whirring in the hillside orchards, in the hilldwarfed trees,
Flapping the rusted roofing off a shed:
If wind were a smell
This would be odor of illness
In a room beyond all power of human cleansing:
I make a place now where
Anything can happen,
Where the spooled snake and the snowy owl may wed.

But I shall not sing the marriage song of that, nor
Of the monster stag stinking of rut
In the bracken behind the widow's cabin, nor
Of the rabiesquinseyed cretin clawing toward the young girl's bed;
I shall not cross the valley to where a moron is climbing the stair,
(A youngster of griseous eye and a cornstalk shock of hair)
Fondling a screwdriver daggerwise
Hulking up to his mother's lair;
I shall not speak of the child whose brain was trowelled by fever,
Nor tell what he did as a man to his wife and daughter,
Nor whisper of the suicide under Black Bridge,
Where the cuckold's wife stabbed herself in the groin, back, and head.
I shall not talk of the bewildered preacher, who cured
Several of his flock in his large smokeshed;

For you want the packaged job:
The linear razzledazzle that

In tying up loose ends
Mummifies dread; that
Takes the terror out of being close:
You want me to take your mind off
The well made plot
Somebody who cares is going to see
You get one
Of these days:
The Poet's Jacinth is good for the stinging of serpents;
And seeds of peony
Being drunk with wine
Are a remedy against the Black Night Mare:

I let my measures warrant themselves;
It isn't my job to salve your case of the Great Bugbear;
I am no Jackanapes of Distancing Assurance,
No bawd with a dose to give you
Something to fear:
But if you have come this far
You may rest with me, now,
Right
Here.